50+ BMAT Essay

- Designed to be pedago
  from Singapore, the to
  world. Great for both weak ...

- Focused on common essays topics that regularly appear in the BMAT

- Examination-focused for maximum impact without wasting time by looking at the test specifications. Best for the last-minute crammers.

- Free additional online resources provided for owners of this book. Get continually updated resources such as essays, essay plans, practices FREE!

- Comprehensive information to make sure that all essential information is included for the latest BMAT syllabus. Never lose marks due to missing topics again!

- Proven track record with almost a decade in training workshops for the BMAT in many cities. Not written by just anyone, but by people who have been involved in the BMAT.

Why get this book?

This book was specially written by a teacher to help his students do well in the BMAT.

This book is dedicated to the many students who have done well in the BMAT under my tutelage over the years. Many of you have moved on to do great things in your medical studies and I'm sure you be will become great physicians in the future.

But forever remember this,

Primum non nocere.

About the author

This BMAT book is designed by Mr Ivan Gn, an experienced teacher in the top performing education system of Singapore, as part of the course to prepare students for the BMAT.

Ivan has been coaching students individually for the BMAT since 2009 who graduated from Imperial College London with a first-class honours degree and formerly taught for many years. He worked as a teacher in Singapore, one of the most successful education systems in the world.

He has conducted classes for the BMAT for several years in different cities such as Singapore, Bangkok, Jakarta, Shanghai and Hong Kong, and has completed a version of the test itself as part of his work. Students who have attended his classes have performed above the BMAT international average and many of them were offered interviews for NTU-Imperial LKCMedicine, Imperial College London as well as Cambridge and Oxford.

Visit our BMAT website at **www.bmat.sg** for extra free resources, more details and practice options.

Contents

Introduction to the BMAT

Why is the BMAT important?

The BMAT is used for admissions into the top United Kingdom universities for various courses, including medicine, veterinary and biomedical courses. It is also used by the Singapore's Nanyang Technological University-Imperial College Lee Kong Chian School of Medicine (LKCMedicine) as well as several top medical universities in Thailand for admission.

The BMAT constitutes a significant component of the composite score for many universities, in additional to the primary qualifications such as the 'A'-Level or IB diploma. It is well-understood by insiders that the BMAT scores are as important as the primary qualifications in terms of the weight, but differs from university to university. A significantly good BMAT score will give you a very important advantage over other candidates when applying for courses in each of the universities around the world.

The Section 3 score is also often used as a tie-breaker to help schools discern students who are better at communication, better clarity of thought and better students who have a higher rates of success.

BMAT Section 3: Writing Task

A selection of four tasks will be available, from which one must be chosen. These will include brief questions based on topics of general, medical, veterinary or scientific interest.

Questions will provide a short proposition and may require candidates to:

- explain or discuss the proposition's implications;
- suggest a counter proposition or argument;
- suggest a (method for) resolution.

The Writing Task provides an opportunity for candidates to demonstrate the capacity to consider different aspects of a proposition, and to communicate them effectively in writing. Skills to be assessed include those concerning communication, described above. All specified skills may be assessed. The question paper will brief candidates about the nature and purpose of the Task. They will be required to produce a written communication, without the assistance of a dictionary or automated spelling and grammar checking software. Whilst they may make preliminary notes, the final product is strictly limited to one A4 page, to promote the disciplined selection and organisation of ideas, together with their concise, accurate and effective expression. When scoring responses, consideration will be given to the degree to which candidates have: addressed the question in the way demanded; organised their thoughts clearly; expressed themselves using concise, compelling and correct English; used their general knowledge and opinions appropriately. Admitting institutions will be provided with a copy of the applicant's response.

	Minutes
TOTAL	30

How is the BMAT Section 3 scored?

Essay marks are awarded separately for the quality of content and quality of English.

BMAT Essay Marking Criteria – quality of content

In arriving at the score for quality of content, markers are instructed to consider:

- Has the candidate addressed the question in the way demanded?
- Have they organised their thoughts clearly?
- Have they used their general knowledge and opinions appropriately?

Scores are awarded on a scale from 1 to 5.

Score 1

An answer that has some bearing on the question but which does not address the question in the way demanded, is incoherent or unfocussed.

Score 2

An answer that addresses most of the components of the question and is arranged in a reasonably logical way. There may be significant elements of confusion in the argument. The candidate may misconstrue certain important aspects of the main proposition or its implication or may provide an unconvincing or weak counter proposition.

Score 3

A reasonably well-argued answer that addresses ALL aspects of the question, making reasonable use of the material provided and generating a reasonable counter-proposition or argument. The argument is relatively rational. There may be some weakness in the force of the argument or the coherence of the ideas, or some aspect of the argument may have been overlooked.

Score 4

A good answer with few weaknesses. ALL aspects of the question are addressed, making good use of the material and generating a good counter proposition or argument. The argument is rational. Ideas are expressed and arranged in a coherent way, with a balanced consideration of the proposition and counter proposition.

Score 5

An excellent answer with no significant weaknesses. ALL aspects of the question are addressed, making excellent use of the material and generating an excellent counter proposition or argument. The argument is cogent. Ideas are expressed in a clear and logical way, considering a breadth of relevant points and leading to a compelling synthesis or conclusion.

An answer judged to be irrelevant, trivial, unintelligible or missing will be given a score of 0.

BMAT Essay Marking Criteria - quality of English

In arriving at the score for quality of English, markers are instructed to consider:

Have they expressed themselves clearly using concise, compelling and correct English?

Scores are awarded on a scale from A to E.

Band A – Good use of English.

- fluent
- good sentence structure
- good use of vocabulary
- sound use of grammar
- good spelling and punctuation
- few slips or errors

Band C – Reasonably clear use of English.

- There may be some weakness in the effectiveness of the English.
- reasonably fluent/not difficult to read
- simple/unambiguous sentence structure
- fair range and appropriate use of vocabulary
- acceptable grammar
- reasonable spelling and punctuation
- some slips/errors

Band E – Rather weak use of English.

- hesitant fluency/not easy to follow at times
- some flawed sentence structure/paragraphing
- limited range of vocabulary
- faulty grammar
- regular spelling/punctuation errors
- regular and frequent slips or errors

An essay that is judged to be below the level of an E will receive an X.

Each essay is double marked. For each scale, if the two scores awarded are the same or occupy adjacent positions on the scale, the scores are combined to give the final mark. If there is a larger discrepancy in the scores on either of the two scales, the essay is marked for a third time, and the final mark awarded is checked by the BMAT Assessment Manager.

The composite mark for the quality of English is derived by combining the two scores as follows: AA = A, AC = B, CC = C, CE = D, EE = E. The composite mark for the quality of content is derived by calculating the average of the two scores.

Visit **http://www.bmat.sg** to download free essays!

Section 3: Writing Task

The writing task is allocated 30 minutes, and must be completed within one side of an A-4 sheet of paper. That is typically about 330 words for a student. Most students will be able to complete writing their essays in 15 minutes, allowing another 15 minutes for question selection, essay planning and checking.

Essay Checklist

Each essay is marked by two markers and the average is taken for the final score. If the two scores deviate too far, a third marker is brought in to moderate the score.

The BMAT essay markers are looking for the following in your essays which you should strive to include:

- Has the candidate answered the question?
- Are the terms properly and correctly defined, if required?
- Has the candidate explained the proposition and explained the implications?
- Were there reasonable counter-arguments?
- Were there suggestions of how conflicts between arguments could be resolved?
- Are the thoughts organised clearly?
- Are the arguments logical?
- Is there good use of general knowledge in the essays?
- Have candidates expressed themselves clearing using concise, correct and compelling English.

Essay Selection

Fundamentally, the Section 3 Essay examination is a content examination. While a good command of English is important, it is the substance of your arguments that will get you a high score. To do well, you need to be well-versed in the arguments, for and against, and present them in a good essay. Hence, preparation before the examination is key to success. The more arguments you remember before the examination, the more you can write to get a high score. With good preparation, most students should easily get a Grade 4 and higher.

You will be given a choice of four questions to choose from. Each question is usually a statement, a quote or a paragraph on a philosophical question which you would have to argue for, or against, depending on the question.

Read each question carefully and mark out key details of each question. Every question will have specific instructions for you to define or explain the propositions, and argue your essay in a particular manner. Each essay will always have three components and will require you to argue from multiple points of view. Highlight these clearly to make sure you answer the question.

At least one of the questions will be related to the biomedical field, for example related to medical ethics, animal treatment and use of drugs. It would be useful if you have spent some time reading up articles and various argument on the following themes:

- Patient's Rights
- Affordable healthcare in society
- Ethics in Medicine
- Euthanasia
- Patient consent
- Doctor-assisted suicide
- Use of experimental drugs
- Role of medicine in society
- Animal cruelty
- Nature conservation

You can find some good essay material at the following websites:

- https://www.nhs.uk/using-the-nhs/about-the-nhs/principles-and-values/
- https://www.bma.org.uk/advice/employment/ethics
- https://www.debate.org/debates/
- https://www.procon.org/

Usually there will be a question on science and technology, but not always. Many of these questions are also intentionally tied into biomedical questions, such as use of technology in biomedical science. Science and technology questions are often more general and discuss effect of science and technology on humanity. It would be useful if you have spent some time reading up articles and various argument on the following themes:

- Scientific knowledge
- Advances in biomedical technology
- Science and society
- Science, technology and human development

You can find some good essay material at the following websites:

- https://www.debate.org/debates/
- https://www.procon.org/

You should choose a question which you are comfortable with and able to do all the following:

1. Define the terms required in the question confidently;
2. Generate least three ideas in favour of the argument;
3. Generate least three ideas against the argument;
4. Provide one example for each idea where applicable.

Essay Structure and Style

It is challenging to prove to the examiners how good you are while keeping to the page limit of one side of the A-4 sized sheet. You would need to be concise, efficient and clear in your language. Do not ramble, go about in circles or use unnecessary words.

We suggest a four-paragraph structure which is simple and easy to fit within the page limit:

1. Introduction and definitions – short, simple, two or three sentences.
2. Arguments for – At least two arguments, good to have one example. Your arguments should be from different points of view where possible (example: legal aspects, practical aspects, cultural aspects). You should also include one implication of the proposition. Typically 4 sentences in this paragraph.
3. Arguments against – Same as arguments for.
4. Conclusion – Analyse both arguments and come to a conclusion with your stand. Resolve conflicts between arguments and propose solutions. About two or three sentences in this paragraph.

So in terms of the number of sentences for each paragraph, it is about 2-4-4-3.

Your sentences should be varied but concise. Long sentences are useful to link arguments together but can be difficult to read. Students also tend to put too many ideas in a long sentence. Shorter sentences are clearer and concise, but result in choppy essays if overused.

Avoid jargons, technical abbreviations and big words unless you absolutely need to. While marks are given for good language, the ability to communicate your ideas clearly are more important.

Be confident in your arguments and do not use ambiguous words and sentences. Sentences such as "I believe that the assertion is flawed because…" show more confidence in your arguments as compared to "The assertion might be wrong…"

It is important that your essay is writing in correct English. Be mindful of your grammar and sentence structures to provide for an easy-to-read essay. Varied sentence structures, good use of vocabulary, proper use of grammar and correct spelling will help you get a good essay score.

Sample Essays

When treating an individual patient, a physician must also think of the wider society.

Explain the reasoning behind this statement. Argue that a doctor should only consider the individual that he or she is treating at the time. With respect to medical treatment, to what extent can a patient's interests differ from those of the wider population?

The field of medicine is one of responsibilities; to patients, the profession, and wider society. At times, these responsibilities may come into conflict, most notably that of a physician's duty to their patients versus their duty to society. This conflict arises from a physician's duty to both heal and prevent disease. By acting in a way that promotes the health of society they promote the health of their future patients. This argument rarely convinces the patient sitting across from the physician and it could be argued that it should not, as the physician-patient relationship is perceived as one of singular consideration.

The "oath of office" for physicians includes a promise to cause no harm, nor allow for harm to come to their patients through inaction. This statement exists not only to guide the morals of physicians, but to inform patients what they can expect when they seek treatment. The idea of patient advocacy is born from the idea of causing harm through inaction. Physicians are compelled to seek the best care for their patients and to overcome barriers that are preventing the acquisition of that care. To consider limiting treatment of one patient for the greater good of society appears to violate this oath of advocacy and potentially weakens the therapeutic relationship between provider and patient. While extreme, the classic example of this is the Tuskeegee Syphilis Experiment; the treatment of one group of patients was knowingly limited to complete a study that defined the most effective treatment for syphilis; this saved countless healthcare dollars, but created an ethical dilemma that retold even today.

Our ability to predict the future has historically been poor in the medical field. Treatments that were thought to be promising are revealed as worthless, while therapies we dismiss become standard of care. To limit a patient's care based on what we think is best for society, in the present day, may be doing them a disservice in the future. A classic example is the use of CT-Scanning to detect lung cancer, a disease that is the 3rd leading cancer by mortality in the united states. Historically thought as "too expensive" and a burden on the healthcare system, CT scanning has been revealed to be a cost-effective way to reduce the risk of lung cancer in long-time smokers.

Given these concerns, are there still benefits for expanding the idea of physician advocacy to all of society? An oft cited example are healthcare concerns of society that effect a physician's individual patient. Vaccinations of the community, preventing the patient family from acquiring disease. Antibiotic stewardship, ensuring the patients family members are not exposed to resistant bacteria. Up to effective mental health interventions for the community, increasing the safety of the community in which the patient's family lives.

While the above examples may not be seen as detrimental to the physician's patients, closer consideration reveals otherwise. Vaccinations can cause personal illness and injury, however minor. Limiting antibiotics will result in some curable disease being missed. And physician participation in mental health interventions will take time, potentially limiting appointments for the individual patient.

These are all examples of how the interests of the individual may conflict with the needs of the wider population. These variations are of course based on a theoretical patient and many may not apply to a patient in reality. As such there may well be room to treat the individual while considering wider society without running afoul of medical ethics.

With limited resources and increasing demand, doctors will not in the future be concerned about how to cure, so much as whether to cure.

Write a unified essay in which you address the following: Explain what you think this statement means. What factors might contribute to 'limited resources' and 'increasing demand'. Advance an argument that governments should ensure that resources for medical care should always match demand.

In the near future, the medical profession may be faced with a new reality, due to increasing demand and limited resources, we may no longer wonder how to cure but who we should cure. Simply put, increases in population, novel treatments, and a continuing shortage of physicians is leading to a world where we can cure the majority of disease, but no longer have time to do so.

The population of the world has been increasing at an exponential rate; advances in sanitation, medicine, and farming have only increased the rate of growth. This growth is augmented by the increasing global life expectancy, it is estimated that by 2020 over 30% of the world's population will be considered "elderly." These factors are major components of the increasing demand for modern medical care. The idea that we must decide who to treat is present even today. Organ transplants, dialysis, proton beam therapy, and many other novel treatments are incredibly limited in supply, there is no reason to assume the great treatments of tomorrow will be any different.

These novel medical treatments are becoming increasingly expensive due to the technology and effort that goes into researching them. Developing a new therapy can cost corporations billions of dollars, requiring massively high prices to recoup said costs. This creates an artificial limitation in supply, only the rich can afford novel treatments as only they can pay for them. Even if a price is set to the lowest possible quantity, while still allowing for recovery of development costs, many individuals will still be "priced out" of healthcare by the bare necessity of requiring a profit to continue further research.

Profit is a key driving force for doctors as well, many are attracted to the medical profession by the promise of a fulfilling job, with good pay, and even better job security. This attraction is not enough to create a healthy physician workforce; many factors go into the training of physicians, well equipped hospitals, competent teachers, monolithic libraries, and copious testing. The facilities to train such students take time to prepare, as such we are facing a massive physician shortage worldwide with no end in sight.

The weight of these issues has been placed on many organizations throughout the history of the medical profession. Yet the one most equate with a duty to act is the government, whether it be that of a nation, state, or city. People consider the government responsible for resource allocation and providing a guiding vision for the people. The base idea of a government is to protect its citizens and act in their best interest. Who then is more responsible, or better equipped, to guarantee sufficient resources for the healthcare of the people.

A well-run government could act to cut costs for research and development through tax breaks and grants. Build up the physician workforce by cutting the red tape that surrounds opening new schools and training hospitals. They could work to better educate the public about the health effects of aging, working to keep seniors healthy and out of the medical system. Not all countries have the luxury of a government that is by the people and for the people; those who do should work towards efficient systems of health and wellbeing. Both for their own good and to act as examples to those who follow.

With limited resources and increasing demand, doctors will not in the future be concerned about how to cure, so much as whether to cure.

Explain what you think this statement means. What factors might contribute to "limited resources" and "increasing demand?" Advance an argument that governments should ensure that resources for medical care should always match demand.

The above statement can be interpreted as follows: soon, healthcare providers will be faced with difficult decisions regarding whether or not to use limited healthcare resources to treat patients in need. Essentially, in the future, healthcare providers will have to determine whether or not it is appropriate to use healthcare resources to administer care to individual patients. Currently, independent of age, race, background and quality of life, every patient receives the same level of healthcare. However, due to limited resources in the future, that may not be the case. Healthcare providers may have to differentiate patients and, ultimately, determine whether or not to treat them.

One of the biggest factors contributing to the scarcity of healthcare resources is the ever-growing global population. The global population has grown exponentially in the past several decades and research indicates the population will only continue to grow in the future. Currently, healthcare resources are already being stretched to their limits, which can only mean one thing for the future generations: limited healthcare resources. Another factor contributing to the scarcity of healthcare resources is the declining number of primary career physicals. Over the last few years, the number of individuals graduating from medical school has declined significantly, leaving a void that does not seem to be filling anytime soon. The individual healthcare provider may be the most important available healthcare resource and with a lack of graduating physicians, fewer people will have an opportunity to gain access to healthcare. With that said, how can healthcare meet the ever increasing demands of those seeking treatment? For some the answer to that question is simple: government intervention.

Those who support government intervention argue the following: in the future, healthcare must be supported by individual governments. Governments must subsidize healthcare and ensure there are available healthcare resources to meet the demands of their citizen populations. After all, one of the roles of a government is to allocate resources, obtained and provided for through taxation, to support their populations. There is no bigger resource than healthcare. Thus, governments must intervene to ensure there will be a sufficient supply of healthcare resources to meet the demands of their citizens. Without government intervention, healthcare resources could dwindle to record low levels, which, in turn, could lead to civil unrest. Essentially, if individuals cannot receive healthcare, they could riot and revolt, leading to destruction and political upheaval. On the other side of the coin, those who do not support government intervention simply argue that healthcare is not a service which should be supported by the government because it is indeed a product just like anything else - individuals can afford it/have access to it or they cannot. Although both sides of the argument are compelling, it may simply come down to an unrealistic expectation. Supply may not always match demand. It is an ebb and flow, which can change with time. Perhaps the best case scenario is somewhere in between, with individual governments and the healthcare industry working together to support resources and treat those in need.

Individual freedom and the rule of law are mutually incompatible.

Write a unified essay in which you address the following:

What might be the grounds for making this assertion? Give a reasoned argument against the proposition. How can the concepts of freedom and law be reconciled in a real society?

The statement 'Individual freedom and the rule of law are mutually incompatible' presents anarchy in opposition to the universal concept of living under obedience to rules governed, in general, by the state. A statement such as this may be made by those for whom a set of laws has proved preventative to their actions. The revolutionary, for example, who believes that the ends justify the means and who takes actions into their own hands, given the end they hope to achieve. In contrast those who uphold the law often cite the fact (in agreement with this statement) that they are happy to be restricted in their personal freedoms for society to function. How this balancing act is achieved has been the subject of much of history.

How we define freedom will determine our reaction to this statement. If individual freedom simply means that I, as an individual, should be able to perform any action I so choose, without the consequence of punishment, then it stands that such a freedom would be incompatible to living under the rule of law. However, if we view individual freedom within the context of wider society, and the mutual benefits of co-operation, then the notion of freedom takes on a much wider scope and can be reconciled to the rule of law. I may not be able to carry out every action I desire, but in limiting myself within the confines of an established law, created in co-operation with others, then I am free within the confines of a system created for mutual benefit.

Nevertheless, such a system creates difficulties when the desires of individuals to certain freedoms falls outside of the law. Take for example current debates over free speech, is it my right to say and think as I wish, even if it causes grave offence? As in George Orwell's 1984 do freedoms stop at acts, or do they spill over into thoughts as well?

What is struck, despite the criticism above, is a balancing act between individual freedom and human flourishing, which throughout history has weighed one way or the other (generally in the direction of the law). The statement is therefore open to abuse by either side. The individual may demand too much freedom, a fact which has a detrimental effect upon others, whilst in opposition the state (which is generally the arbiter of law) may curtail freedoms to the point of oppression.

In a real society, what is required is an implicit form of social contract between citizen and state. A contract which gives rights and freedoms to the individual whilst safeguarding the well-being of all under a general rule of law. Such a social contract could only be limited to the curtailment of actions, since to deny individuals the freedom to think in a way they wish would stray into totalitarianism. In contrast, allowing certain thoughts to spill over into action could create anarchy. We must therefore carefully define freedom before we can situate it within the context of law and order, if this is achieved then the two are no longer mutually incompatible.

Democratic freedom means there should be no restriction on what may be said in public.

Explain what you think democratic freedom means. Argue that there should be restrictions on what is said in public. To what extent do you agree that there should be limitations on what can be said in public?

The issues surrounding 'freedom of speech' are currently a hot topic of debate. Should an individual be free to say whatever they wish in whatever circumstances without regard to the ways in which what they say will impact upon others or more specifically those to whom they refer? The adage that 'sticks and stones may break my bones, but words will never hurt me' has, in recent years, been proved wrong as offence has been publicly taken by individuals against others who criticise them or their lifestyles.

Democratic freedom is consistently held up as the political state par excellence, in which an individual is free, within the confines of law, to act and do as they please. Such a state implies freedom of words as well as actions. Though we might argue that democracy only allows us to vote in a representative who may speak for us in the public sphere, our own personal views devolved to them. But even in such a free society restrictions are placed upon many of the actions we perform. For example: I cannot steal or physically harm without experiencing consequences if I am caught. As a society, we punish wrong action but we are still unsure how to punish what is perceived to be wrong speech or thought, we call it a democratic right to speak our mind.

To restrict the freedom of speech would appear to be undemocratic, I may not like what a person has to say yet surely they have a right to say it and I, in turn, have the right to reply? Do words hurt in the same way that a bullet does? On the face of it we may say no, but take the following examples: a preacher of hate against the West who fires up a young zealot to go out and kill hundreds in a terrorist atrocity or the white supremacist who gives a speech condemning immigration and incites racist riots as a result. Whilst words may not in themselves be problematic the actions they lead to may well be. The pen is mightier than the sword and in these cases it is clearly right to restrict such speech for the good of all. Conversely it may be argued that anyone should be able to say anything they wish for the simple fact that this allows for open and honest debate, despite the consequences.

A balance therefore is required between allowing free and proper debate, and yes this will mean at times causing offence, and the restriction of the type of speech which can inflame and lead to violence. If, as a society, we reach a point in which merely 'causing offence to another' is deemed a crime then we have reached the point where democratic freedom is lost. Limitations to speech should only be imposed where there is a tangible and real threat that what is said will lead to actual physical harm (and what constitutes harm?). But despite all this the greatest tool of democracy invented in recent years: the internet, will continue to allow the dissemination of opinion of every shade, and thus free speech, and its effects, will continue.

Science only tells us what is possible, not what is right.

Explain what this statement means. Argue to the contrary that science helps us to judge what is right. To what extent can decisions about what is right and wrong be informed by science?

The question of how we determine what is right or wrong is an ancient one; and through the ages many different approaches have been taken in determining moral decisions. For much of human history the answers to such questions were determined by recourse to Natural Law, or an absolutism based upon divine inspiration. In our modern age, many people have turned to alternative sources as a basis for moral guidance, science being one of them. With its emphasis upon objectively discoverable truths, based upon empirical evidence, an argument can be made for science being a means by which the good can be determined. For example, in the fight against disease is it permissible to alter embryos or even abort them if they show signs of hereditary conditions which would be better off eliminated from the human gene pool? Science, and its medical subsidiaries, would probably argue yes based solely upon the evidence; whilst those of a different persuasion may well suggest it is not permissible to tamper with nature in this way.

The statement 'Science only tells us what is possible, not what is right' opens up a range of possible interpretations. From a non-moral perspective, we may view this as a statement about facts and errors. Science may, to the best of our current knowledge, offer a particular explanation for this or that phenomenon, this does not necessarily mean it is ultimately correct. There have been many examples of scientific 'fact' altering when new discoveries are made. In these cases, science shows us only the possibility of what may be right, and not a definitive truth. Though most scientists would surely argue that there are many things that we do know for certain.

To return to the moral dimension of this statement, the above example of eliminating disease would seem to be one way in which science can help us to judge what is right. In other cases, scientific proofs could show the danger of a particular course of environmental action, or of the potential effects of developing new weapons. All of these discoveries have an ethical dimension to them, and just because we can do something does not mean that we should.

Whilst there is a limit as to how science can lead us to judge what is right or wrong, the evidence it provides can be a considerable factor in determining our course of action. By its very definition science is foundationally objective, it produces empirical results which are then open to interpretation. Ultimately though it is our own moral compass – the basis of which is the result of many factors – which determines our course of action. Science may say that aborting children with a disease which is easily transmitted would ensure the survival of others, but it is up to me to use that evidence to make a judgement about termination. In a case such as this scientific discovery provides an impetus, but other factors determine the outcome.

Science can provide an objective basis of evidence in order to determine moral direction. It cannot say specifically what is right or wrong. Nevertheless, possibility in itself can often be enough to sway our moral compass, and thus science informs us of right and wrong to a considerable extent.

Doubt is not a pleasant condition, but certainty is absurd.

Explain what this statement means. Argue to the contrary that to be certain about something is not necessarily absurd. To what extent do you agree with Voltaire?

As a philosopher Voltaire was no doubt acutely aware of the difficulty of being certain of anything hence this statement arising. Can I be certain that the room I am sitting in exists? Can I be certain that 2+2=4 and so on. To claim that something is certain is to make a bold statement about reality. As human beings, we like to think that what we know is correct, indeed much of our day to day activity is based upon numerous underlying assumptions. For example, that the sun will rise tomorrow and there will be daylight. Such assumptions are so imbedded that we do not give them a second thought. But if upon reflection we realise that we cannot be certain of any fact, and thus exist in a state of perpetual doubt, then this indeed is not a pleasant thought, it's positively nihilistic. But is it true to suggest that being certain about something is absurd?

Whilst the sceptic may ponder whether the room they are sitting in exists or not upon leaving they will take the door rather than leap from the window – just to be safe. Scepticism often comes to an end when we are faced with reality. To function we must accept that we live within a world in which many things are as they appear, and should be used accordingly. In the above example I take the door, and this implies that I am reasonably certain it is the right thing to do.

Whilst empirical 'certainties' can often be called into question; the certainties of mathematics are rather different. 2+2 would = 4 whether anyone was alive to think it or not, it is a rational rather than empirical certainty and one which we would be more inclined to agree with than disagree. In this case certainty is not absurd, there are simply no counter examples to show that adding two objects together will not produce four objects.

Despite these counter arguments to Voltaire's statement, there is considerable truth in what he says. I am caught within a system which demands me to accept as certain many things around me, I can doubt all I like, but in order to get on in life I must accept certain things as true even though I have never experienced them for myself and on one level this is absurd. The definition of 'certainty' must therefore change if we are to avoid the angst of constant doubt. It is not necessarily that something is a fact (particularly in terms of empiricism) but that I must accept it as a truth in each situation and act accordingly.

But ultimately a healthy dose of doubt is no bad thing. To question reality, or more pointedly that which others claim to be true, is the basis of reasoned thinking. We may not need to wallow in angst over doubt, but questioning that which is certain can only lead us closer to the truth.

Irrationally held truths may be more harmful than reasoned errors.

Write a unified essay in which you address the following:

This is a statement concerning truth in science; explain what you think it means. From what Huxley says in this statement, what do you think he means by irrationally held truths? Advance a contrary argument, that reasoned errors are more harmful than irrationally held truths.

Huxley's statement that 'Irrationally held truths may be more harmful than reasoned errors' is a complex one. If something is true then surely it is rational? At least if it is objectively true. And how do we define a 'reasoned error'? Is this not a contradiction in terms, since reason should not lead us into error?

But many so called 'truths' are not necessarily reasonably held, we accept them because others tell us, or we read them in a book. 'The earth is round, and not flat' may be one such example. Standing on the level ground, or looking out from a mountain top, would give me no reason to think otherwise, I have never been into space and seen the world as a sphere. In this case a reasoned error: that I see a flat world around me and therefore it is flat, seems more plausible than stating that the earth is round because others have told me so, and I have looked it up in a book. Whilst there are many things that I can hold to be true because of my reasoning, that 2+2=4 for example, there are also many things I take to be true that I do not have first-hand experience of and it is this fact that Huxley refers to in his statement.

One scientifically irrational truth might be to suggest that the earth was formed millions of years ago, that dinosaurs came first and so on. We have evidence for this, but it is still not first hand. My rationality (which is generally limited by personal experience) could suggest its truth, but I am bound by the limitations of external factors in determining the actual truth of the proposition.

In opposition, a reasoned error might be to suggest that the Earth is only so many thousand years old. The reasoning attached to this being that the Bible says so, my personal beliefs tell me and throughout history this has been the predominant view. Within its sphere this is a reasoned error, based upon a framework of inter-consistent views.

For Huxley, these irrationally held truths may be more harmful than reasoned errors because they dispense with the necessity of independent thinking. If I simply accept the theory of evolution, without investigating it for myself then I have blinded myself in terms of the true acquisition of knowledge.

But this factor also provides a considerable argument as to why reasoned errors are more harmful than irrationally held truths, for the simple fact that their proponents have a framework of belief within which the error has been constructed. The earth, and its inhabitants, may well have come about through evolution, but if I believe this blindly and come across a creationist with a strong framework upon which to base their argument, my own could easily fall down and I may be forced to admit that they have provided a more reasoned argument for their error than I have for my irrational truth. My view may well be correct, but without reasonability to uphold it I am left only with opinion.

Our zeal to make things work better will not be our anthem: it will be our epitaph.

Write a unified essay in which you address the following:

The above statement was made in reference to modern technology; explain what you think it means. Advance an argument against the statement above, i.e. in support of the proposition our zeal to make things work better will be our anthem.

This statement arouses thoughts of millennial disaster theories or action movies in which the world is saved with only minutes to spare. It is an emotive statement, which acts within the broader article as a rallying call for a reassessment of humanity's attitude towards science and modern technology, which the author argues will ultimately destroy us.

The world is becoming ever more reliant upon technology; and automation has seen many jobs, once done by men and women, now controlled by machine, leading to a loss of work and income, and the potential economic unrest which this brings. Our technology also allows us not only to achieve more but also to kill and maim more effectively, the current crisis on the Korean peninsula a case in point. With greater industrialisation comes the threat of environmental and accidental disaster, and as man encroaches ever more upon the planet's resources it could be argued that our time is running out. It is for these reasons, and many more, that Appleyard makes this statement, and accuses progress, veiled as something to be desired, to be that which will bring an end to humanity.

Such a view was particularly prevalent around the turn of the 20th century, the subject of much science fiction. But if we look past the sensationalist headlines there are a several reasons for discounting Appleyard's statement.

Whilst human progress may well be causing potential damage in the short term, it is also creating much good. The continuation of scientific and technological discoveries will no doubt solve many of the issues surrounding environmental damage and health, and whilst automation may be taking jobs away from manual labourers, the advent of the internet has created endless opportunities for work on an international scale.

For all of us death is a certainty, and we know that ultimately the world itself will cease to exist, with such thoughts we may question the value of any progress at all. Nevertheless, far from signalling our demise, progress in the future will almost certainly provide opportunities for the human race itself to survive, despite our planet's potential destruction. Technology may well be our salvation rather than our epitaph.

On an individual level, the progress of technology continues to provide health benefits for all, we live longer and enjoy greater well-being, what once routinely killed is now routinely cured, at a personal level progress allows many to change their own epitaph and live a longer more fulfilling life.

With these arguments in mind it is clear that far from being our end technology and progress may well signal our survival. Instead of death it has the potential to provide a greater quality of life for all and a future not dependent upon the world around us.

Science is not a follower of fashion nor of other social or cultural trends.

Explain what you think the statement means. Argue to the contrary. To what extent do you agree with the statement?

At face value, this statement would appear to be correct. If one views science as a means of discovery and progress, and a discipline which prides itself on 'seeking after truth' from the standpoint of objectivity and fact, then science should be largely unaffected by current trends and influences. Indeed, to remain objective it should be. The one who makes such a statement would argue that for science to provide us with the truth it must be free from exterior influence and agenda. Allowed to make discoveries, however controversial they may be.

Many of the greatest scientific discoveries would not have taken place if this had not been the case. For example, when all around him believed the earth to be at the centre of the universe, Galileo postulated the theory that in fact the earth revolves around the sun. If he had followed the cultural trends of the time then this theory would never have arisen.

But several arguments can be presented, in contradiction to the idea that science is not a follower of fashion and cultural trends. Firstly, science often reacts to the situations and problems presented by the world. Take, for example, the AIDs epidemic. If human beings had not contracted the AIDs virus from chimps then the massive push to eradicate its spread and develop treatments for it would never have taken place. The apes would simply have been left to die but instead science presented a solution.

A second example may be found in environmental science. With the rapid decline in fossil fuels new, alternative energy sources were required, and science responded to this with a raft of new technologies designed to harvest natural energy. Had fossil fuels not been running low, and the earth heading for environmental disaster, then such a development would not have taken place.

At a more superficial level we see science deployed in the development of new beauty products, types of food, means of entertainment, and leisure opportunities as the demand of those who use such things increases. Virtual reality being a current topic of interest alongside the desire to travel further and faster. It could be argued that science has always followed current trends and fashions, as a slave to their development, rather than as a follower. Such a fact is important given the limited resources available, and because these developments may only benefit certain sectors of society. Equally it means that humanity gains that which it wants from science and, if objective scientific research is still to be carried out, science needs to demonstrate that it can also meet the demands asked of it.

Whilst many fundamental scientific theories, such as evolution, or the spherical earth, would not have been possible had their proponents not risked everything to go against cultural and social trends. At the level of development, and the response to human situations, science is very much a follower (if not led) by the trends of the day. Science must be both a pioneer of new theories and a help to current trends and ideas if it is to remain both objectively useful and a challenger to convention.

You can resist an invading army; you cannot resist an idea whose time has come.

Explain the reasoning behind this statement. Argue that, on the contrary, any idea can be suppressed with sufficient force. What do you think gives power to an idea?

It is said that 'the pen is mightier than the sword,' a statement like that made by Victor Hugo. The point he makes is that progress is an inevitability, that when an idea, which is found to be correct, has come to fruition, its eventual acceptance is guaranteed. An invading army can be fought against and defeated, with enough man power and resources. But if an idea arises, even one never considered before, or previously considered as preposterous, and if that idea garners support and acceptance, resistance towards it is futile. Ideas can be much more powerful than any foreign invader, the political science of Marx and Marxism being one example.

Whilst an idea can gain popular support, and spread, without hope of suppression, such a fact is not an inevitability. History has often shown that ideas can be suppressed with sufficient force. For example, under Communism propaganda and violence were used to ensure that ideas relating to freedom and democracy could not gain popular support. And today laws relating to the prevention of terrorism are ensuring that certain ideas, despite their potential popularity, cannot be disseminated widely for fear that they could lead to violence, their proponents arrested and detained. In these cases, force is used to suppress ideas because they are considered objectively dangerous by those in authority, for good or ill.

But it is not just physical force than can be used to suppress populist ideas. At times throughout history different scientific theories, now known to be right, have been ruthlessly suppressed through contrary reasoning. Evolution and geocentrism being two examples. In these cases, alternative, and long held theories, were used to supress that which is now known to be true. Such manipulation is seen today in the phenomena of 'fake news', ideas can always be supressed if they are dangerous. Nevertheless, Hugo suggests that ideas have 'their time' and in reality the truth will always come out.

Ideas are given power in a variety of ways, firstly they must be disseminated to reach as many people as possible, they must have popular appeal and attract attention, they must be relevant to the issues of the day, and attract a wide following. In our modern age ideas can spread from one corner of the planet to the next in a split second, harnessing this ability also gives power to an idea. Ironically it is often those ideas which others try to supress which in themselves become the most popular. If a book is banned then people who may never have heard of it will desire to read it. Likewise, an idea supressed by force can often be the one which ends up being most popular, democratic ideas in the Soviet Union, for example. Whilst ideas can be resisted, ultimately they are mightier than any invading army.

That which can be asserted without evidence, can be dismissed without evidence.

Explain what you think Christopher Hitchens means. Argue to the contrary that some assertions do not require evidence. To what extent do you agree with the statement?

Christopher Hitchens is well known for his views in the debate between science and religion, from which this statement may be drawn. In it he suggests that an assertion which is not backed up by evidence can be dismissed with no recourse to further dialogue. If I say that 'the world is flat' and provide no evidence to prove this: a set of pictures, a journey into space, a textbook of evidence etc, then my statement can be dismissed without further arguments.

For Hitchens, an assertion is not enough to warrant another to believe what I have said. Any statement must be confirmed by evidence in support. If I am to say that 2+2=4 then I must provide examples where two objects added to two objects produce four objects, and so on. On face value such a statement appears reasonable, but whilst the need for evidence is clear, should we immediately dismiss a statement not backed up by other sources, without even arguing the case?

The statement as given does not provide an answer as to what constitutes evidence. Could another person support my claim, even if it were false, or could a false assertion be made within a system which itself is false but which provides additional 'evidence' to support the initial claim? In addition, not all assertions require evidence to back them up, instead we often make inferences without firm evidence.

Examples of this can be found in science. If I know that the human heart pumps blood around the body, and I encounter a new species of animal with similar characteristics, then it is reasonable to infer that that animal has a heart. Equally if I know that fish breathe with gills then it is reasonable to infer that a new species of fish will do so too. In these cases, I do not need quantifiable evidence to infer a truth.

From a personal perspective, I may make the claim that I carried out such and such an action many years ago. There may be no evidence for this but equally there is no reason to doubt it. If I told someone that I visited London in 2004 there would be no reason for them to require me to prove this fact, if I told them I had been to the Moon the opposite would be true.

Even if we agree with Hitchens' statement, we should be wary of dismissing another's assertion without providing evidence of our own. In an intellectual debate we do not prove our point to be right by not engaging with the other party. If a person falls into error, and makes an assertion without evidence, our job should be to counter that statement with evidence to the contrary. This is so that the objective truth is discovered by both parties, because when discussing the same subject it is possible that both sides may have something to contribute. Equally everyday life is made up of assertions and whilst it may be possible to provide evidence for them, there would be no reason to doubt them and require it.

When you can measure what you are speaking about, and express it in numbers, you know something about it; but when you cannot ... your knowledge is of a meagre and unsatisfactory kind.

Explain what you think Lord Kelvin means. In particular discuss the extent to which Lord Kelvin's remark applies to biology and medicine, with specific examples of topics that do or do not require to be treated quantitatively.

This statement argues that if a particular piece of information is not quantifiable, or backed up with figures, then its validity is of a dubious nature. Without a set of data, which can be measured against other gathered evidence, any conclusion will be unsatisfactory.

Biologists often seek to classify their findings, and thus use Kelvin's assertion as a means of proof. For example: cataloguing the number of species found in a given environment. This allows them to assess whether a species is native or an outsider. If a portion of rainforest is analysed and found to contain hundreds of one particular bird then it can be claimed that this bird is native. If, however, only one example of a poisonous frog is catalogued then the species could be classified foreign to the environment. In this case quantity offers the basis for knowledge. This approach would apply to many areas of biology such as the genetic make-up of a person or assessing whether an animal is an herbivore. At a superficial level Kelvin's statement is simply a matter of drawing conclusions through multiple observations.

Another example can be found in medicine, and specifically in medical studies relating to drugs. Every new drug is tested before it can be used universally. Doctors will note the potential side effects in a random sample of test cases. If 5 out of 10 people who take the newly developed drug experience severe flu like symptoms then it can be reasonably claimed that the drug is likely to cause a fifty percent chance of flu in those who use it. In contrast, if the sample is of 200 people, and one experiences a severe nose bleed a day later, then this would not count as evidence that the drug can cause nose bleeds in those who use it. In this case quantifiable evidence will be used to assess the effects of the drug.

Despite these examples it seems overly dismissive of Kelvin to suggest that any theory, not backed up by numbers and quantity, is of a dubious nature. Often one theory leads from another and this is how discoveries are made. I may be certain of a fact but I should always be open to the possibility that it could be wrong. The example of a new illness is a case in point. If a doctor has observed multiple patients exhibiting X and Y symptoms in a disease, but is then confronted with a patient showing X, Y and Z symptoms, rather than dismissing this observation, he should at least consider it as a new effect of the disease. This may give rise to further observations of the same kind.

In Biology, it is not necessary to always observe things quantitively. If a biologist dissects an animal they do not necessarily need to dissect another hundred examples of the species to know the anatomy of the subject. Observation alone, rather than multiplying examples, is sufficient in this case. Likewise, assumptions about our biological makeup were made long before Biologists could routinely examine corpses to determine the truth. Whilst quantifying a theory may well give further reason to believe it, the multiplication of numbers does not necessarily tell us that something is truer than we originally thought, it can only serve as further confirmation.

When you want to know how things really work, study them when they are coming apart.

Explain what this statement means. Argue to the contrary. To what extent do you agree with the assertion?

This statement provides an interesting consideration of the way in which things work; and whilst it is perhaps meant to refer to mechanical objects, it could also be applied to natural objects, particularly animals, too. By this assertion William Gibson means that to understand how an object functions we should observe it, either by taking it apart, or watching it fall apart gradually, the latter being more useful for scientific research.

A good example of this would be an investigation into the workings of an old-fashioned pocket watch. On the face of it we see a device used for telling the time, with hands revolving around a face, but how does it work? On the metal casing, there is no indication of the mechanics contained within. It is only when we begin to take it apart, and study the individual components, that we begin to discover the complexity of the internal mechanism, and how each part fits together to produce the whole. Likewise, the art of animal dissection is another way of explaining how a thing works through removing parts of it and examining them. We know, for example, that blood runs around our body, but only by cutting one open do we see the internal pumping method of the heart before us and learn of the similarities between different animals.

Despite its attraction such a method is not the only means by which we discover how things really work. Indeed, the method of 'watching things come apart' can only be applied to certain sections of scientific enquiry. Take astronomy as a case in point. Rather than taking apart a planet, or the solar system, which would be impossible, the astronomer observes how it works by cataloguing phenomena and comparing them to other similar instances. As with other scientific investigations, observation and the repetition of results can tell us precisely what is happening without the need to 'take things apart.' Another example is found in chemistry, in a chemical experiment I do not observe elements coming apart but rather combining to create an effect. If I can repeat this effect X number of times, then I can be certain I know how this experiment works. Likewise, in biology I may dissect an animal to find out what its inner parts look like but I may also observe it, compare it to others similar species and make my assessment based upon these findings alongside other numerical data. Additionally, not every field of study contains things which can come apart and be observed, the mathematician does not understand how a mathematical formula works by taking it apart, this would be nonsensical, instead he studies the formula to reach his conclusion.

Whilst watching things come apart is one effective method of discovering how things work, it is not the only method available. Many branches of science rest upon observation rather than dissection to ascertain results, and often it is the acquisition of numerical data which provides the best idea of how something works. In practice both methods are employed by scientists to reach their results, dependent upon the scientific field of enquiry.

Ignorance more frequently begets confidence than does knowledge: it is those who know little, and not those who know much, who so positively assert that this or that problem will never be solved by science.

Explain what you think is meant by this statement. Argue to the contrary. To what extent do you think it is true?

Scientific study seeks to discover the truth about the world around us, it is constantly evolving as new information is acquired. Whilst some would argue that there is no problem which science will not one-day resolve, others suggest that there are fundamental questions that science cannot ever hope to answer. According to Darwin, those who know little dismiss rigorous scientific enquiry, and its future progress, out of ignorance, or because they are blinded to the truth, perhaps due to religious affiliation or the embracing of alternative theory. The converse implication being that those who know much about scientific enquiry would never make an assertion such as this.

In order to analyse this statement we must first provide an account of what is meant by a scientific problem. If we limit Darwin's statement to a purely objective view of science, one which does not stray into the realms of philosophical enquiry, then a scientific problem is one which arises from the observation of phenomena and the need for explanation and theory of that phenomena. Science asks: 'what physical phenomena occurred when the universe was created?' and not 'why was the universe created?'

But despite Darwin's statement there are those who know a lot about science who could confidently assert that there are problems within it which may never be solved, indeed their expertise may be the basis for this claim. To know a lot about a subject also mean to know its limitations. The astrophysicist may know a great deal about the structures of the universe but they may also know the limitations of their knowledge regarding the basis of these structures, and may confidently assert that they know all they will ever know.

Additionally, a person with considerable scientific knowledge will argue that certain subjects have reached the limitations of knowledge. This may be the case for the biologist who catalogues animals or plants. Once the subject has been fully analysed, and catalogued, then it is unlikely, from a purely scientific perspective, that further problems relating to it would need to be solved.

On the face of it this statement appears somewhat elitist, and an attack on those who make generally sweeping statements, without reference to the facts. But the assertion that the problems of science may never be solved could be made by one who knows a lot or one who knows a little, it all depends upon what they know and to what problems they are referring. Given our definition of science it is questions relating to phenomena which are best answered through scientific investigation. The question 'how was the universe created?' will no doubt one day be solved, but why it was created will remain a mystery due to scientific limitations.

To be ignorantly confident, rather than knowledgeably confident is certainly a disadvantaged state to be in. But to know little rather than to know a lot is not necessarily a barrier to confident assertion in a particular field. I can know only about a specific field of study, whilst confidently asserting its limitations. Whilst another person may hold wide ranging knowledge without any sense of the limitations which that knowledge can accede to.

A scientific man ought to have no wishes, no affections - a mere heart of stone.

Explain what this statement means. Argue that scientific enquiry benefits from personal wishes and affections. To what extent do you think a scientist should have 'a mere heart of stone'?

Darwin's statement that a scientist should 'have no wishes, no affections – a mere heart of stone' is a pronouncement upon the need for objectivity in scientific research and observation. By it he means that in conducting scientific research a scientist should not be influenced by their personal affections or desires. He may also be suggesting that the scientist should place their personal beliefs to one side, for the good of their objective goal.

One such example of this would be a scientist who personally believes that the destruction of the natural habit is having a negative effect upon the planet, if they were charged with investigating new methods of mining fossil fuels (which may have a positive long-term impact) would they set aside their personal beliefs to make an objective study? The question arises: should scientific enquiry reject personal wishes and affections or embrace them?

For the modern scientist, personal wishes and affections are entirely compatible with scientific enquiry. If a scientist wishes to study a topic then they do not require an emotional detachment from it; rather, having an emotional attachment towards it will surely give rise to greater enthusiasm and commitment. If a scientist cares deeply about an issue, such as the safeguarding of the environment, then they cannot help but allow their personal wishes and affections to take hold.

Whilst clearly some scientific research requires no emotional attachment to the subject, geological studies for example, much of science cannot fail but to cause emotional reaction in the one studying it. The scientist who hopes to be the first to contact alien life, for example, or who wishes to safeguard a species from extinction. In these cases, a healthy dose of wishing is no bad thing, if it drives on those keen to make new and remarkable discoveries.

But is Darwin correct to make his assertion, given its time and place? Objectivity in scientific research can, and does, lead to progress. One example is as follows: like it or not drugs, which benefit mankind, are tested upon animals, many of whom die in the process. If scientists had the same respect for other animal life, as they do human life, then such testing would not take place. Possessing a 'heart of stone', or at least a healthy detachment, in this case, is beneficial for the development of drugs since it removes any emotional bonds between scientist and subject.

Darwin himself would have been familiar with the idea of animal dissection and with keeping animals in captivity for study. To keep animals in this way requires a level of emotional detachment from their welfare. But is such a detachment a good thing? Surely it is better for the scientist to care for the welfare of the animals under their charge, not only for their own moral well-being, but also to safeguard against charges of animal cruelty from those involved in animal rights campaigns.

At the time of Darwin this statement was a reasonable one but with advances in technology and a modern understanding of scientific ethics such a view, in its extreme, appears unnecessary and emotional attachment to one's subject seems reasonable and right.

A pet belongs to its owner - it is their property.

Thus, if a client asks for their healthy cat to be painlessly euthanised, a veterinary clinician should always agree to this request. Explain the reasoning behind the statement. Argue to the contrary that a veterinary clinician should never agree to such a request. To what extent should pet owners influence clinicians' decisions?

We would not refer to another human being as 'our property' but it is customary to speak of animals as 'belonging' to an owner. We speak of 'my dog' in the same way that we say: 'my house'. If I own a piece of property, it is my right to get rid of it as I wish. I can sell 'my' house should I wish to do so. I could also destroy my house by burning it to the ground. In these cases, my actions are determined by my own volition, with no recourse to the thing I own.

If ownership is the determining factor in how I view and use the objects which I own then it is reasonable to suggest, as this statement does, that should I wish to euthanise my healthy cat then it is my right to do so. If I can afford to pay the vet's fee, and I should choose to dispose of my property in this way, then that is all that is required for the veterinary clinician to agree to my request and euthanise the cat.

But, unlike inanimate objects, there seems to be something inherently wrong about choosing to dispose of an animal in this way. It is likely that a veterinary clinician would decline my request to euthanise leaving me with two options: keep the cat or dispose of it myself. This is due to the idea that along with human rights, animals also have rights, including the right to life.

Whilst I may have purchased the cat from a breeder and cared for its material needs can it be said to belong to me? Bonds of affection may develop but animals remain independent creatures. If I suddenly ceased to care for an animal I had purchased and released it into the wild then it would have no difficulty in caring for itself. An animal therefore has an autonomy which an inanimate piece of property does not have, it has rights, the right to life being paramount.

Given this autonomy, the veterinary clinician would argue that under no circumstance do they have the right to end a healthy animal's life since, despite its inability to communicate, it would not choose to do so. In a straightforward case of an 'owner' requesting euthanasia it is likely the clinician would never assent.

In addition, given the need to care for genuinely sick animals, the clinician may cite this case as a waste of time and resources when genuine cases require their assistance and such a course of action opens the way for others to demand a similar approach. The possibility of transferring ownership or rehoming the animal without the need to kill may also be suggested. These factors add weight to the idea that a clinician would never countenance euthanasia for a healthy animal

If an animal is found to be sick or suffering then euthanasia is the humane course of action, but a veterinary clinician should never be influenced in this decision by the wishes of the 'owner' but rather on an objective assessment of the suffering of the animal and its innate right to exist. In no circumstance should an animal need to die simply for convenience since it has a right to life.

There is more to healing than the application of scientific knowledge.

Write a unified essay in which you address the following:

Briefly define 'scientific knowledge'. Explain how it might be argued that medical treatment that is not wholly based on scientific knowledge is worthless. Discuss whether there can be approaches to healing that are valid but not amenable to scientific experiment.

In this statement the term 'scientific knowledge' refers to medical science used to heal and cure disease. If I have a headache then I take a paracetamol tablet, the chemicals present in the tablet have been scientifically proven to take away the pain in my head. Thus, in this case, scientific knowledge is applied to healing.

In recent years there has been a surge in so called 'alternative therapies,' though of course such practices have been around since man first attempted to cure disease. These take a myriad of forms such as homeopathy, crystal healing, prayer healing, and so on. In some cases the use of such alternative therapies may well lead to healing but the scientific basis is unproven, and more likely to be the effect of placebo and the individuals belief that the treatment will work. Whilst a cure secured in such a manner would of course be beneficial to the patient any scientific link remains dubious.

If a patient is cured either through an alternative therapy, or the psychological effects which a placebo can have, such an effect adds little to definitive scientific knowledge. It could not be claimed that such an approach would be successful in every case, as it can say for an antibiotic known to kill a particular type of infection every time it is used. If a medical treatment does not have a high chance of working in every case to which it is applied then its usefulness is minimal. Science in general rests upon repeatable and observable patterns and the same is true for medicine. A doctor needs to know that the treatment they give for a particular disease will work in almost all cases of that disease occurring. The worth of alternative therapies continues to be called into question because of this fact.

Nevertheless, we should not discount the powerful psychological effects in those who, having received alternative therapies to those scientifically approved, find themselves healed. The devoutly religious individual who prays hard to be healed and has others pray over them no doubt has strong faith that they will be cured, in certain cases this positive mental attitude is bound to have an effect. On a more scientific basis it may be that a doctor requests that a patient try a new form of drug untested before, one that science is yet to confirm as being effective. The person may be cured, having taken the risk of taking the new and untrialled drug. In this case scientific fact is replaced by a hope that what is thought to work will indeed work.

Whilst the majority of doctors would not endorse non-scientifically proven treatments, their use alongside conventional medication can clearly have beneficial scientific effects. If we believe we will get better then there is more chance of us doing so as we put in more effort and focus on getting the right treatments and proper conduct towards recovery. Likewise it is only recently that we have begun to understand why particular treatments work. In the past 'wise men' or 'women' used plants and herbs to cure those who were sick, they didn't know why they worked but they knew they did. Modern medicine can now explain why particular plants have the effect they were said to have, the willow tree containing aspirin for example. Whilst scientifically proven treatments must continue to be used we should not discount the alternatives for the benefits to well-being which they can derive for us.

Our genes evolved for a Stone Age life style. Therefore, we must adopt Stone Age habits if we are to be healthy.

Write a unified essay in which you address the following:

Explain the logical connexion between the two sentences. What might be the practical implications if we were to agree with the reasoning? Discuss the extent to which the argument is valid.

The study of evolutionary biology has demonstrated that evolution takes place over dramatically long periods of time, as species adapt to their natural environments. Such change can be observed in every type of species, and perhaps most drastically in human beings. As we have traced our ancestry from primitive man to that of today, it has become clear that many of the traits we display have their origin in the evolutionary necessities of the past.

The logical connexion between these two sentences appears reasonable. If we accept evolutionary theory, and the time it takes for change to occur, then it becomes clear that we are little changed from our stone age ancestors. If our genetic attributes are still adapted to suit the lifestyle of the stone age man then surely behaving in this manner would be naturally beneficial to our health and well-being. But do the implications of this connection make sense?

If this were true then we would seek to reject the many advances in technology which have taken place since stone age man walked the earth. We would drastically change our diet, eating only plants and hunted animals neglecting our natural development in taste for new foods and perhaps being unable to stomach that which our ancestors ate, we would eschew the benefits of transport only using our feet on which to get around, and we would no longer benefit from modern medicine or the comforts of home and heating. Our society would become tribal, rather than national, and endeavours in the arts replaced by the constant need to hunt and gather, we would eschew economics in favour of war or theft. A further implication would be that our societal and educational endeavours would suffer, in order to exist as hunter gatherers time for education and human progress would be limited, we would advance far less rapidly than we have done so recently, indeed we would probably regress. Whilst our genes may be that of stone age man our habits have evolved somewhat further.

Whilst we could all benefit from eating a healthier diet, such as that enjoyed by our ancestors, and taking more exercise, in line with their own physical exertions, these facts have less to do with inherited genes and more to do with the fact that diet and exercise are beneficial to health in general. Whilst there is an underlying validity to the argument it is also clear that in adopting such a lifestyle we would also be rejecting much of our wider evolution. One example of this would be in medicine and the treatment of disease, adopting stone age medical practices (which would have been largely non-existent) we would see an instant regress in health, and a dramatic rise in premature death.

Evolution is not just a physical phenomenon but also a social one. We are no longer hunter gatherers existing in a tribal society. It is clear from archaeological records that today we live longer, remain healthier, and enjoy far greater living standards than our stone age ancestors. Whilst our genes may have stone age origins, and we may still be adapted to the possibility of such a lifestyle, the actual living out of it, beyond a simpler diet and taking more exercise, would make us far less healthy than we are today.

A little learning is a dangerous thing.

Explain what you think the author means by this statement. Advance an argument against the statement above, i.e. in support of the proposition 'a little learning is not a dangerous thing'. What do you think determines whether or not learning can be a dangerous thing?

By his statement Alexander Pope could be suggesting one of two things. Either that it is dangerous to know only a small amount about a particular subject and then try to act upon it without having the full picture. Or, more positively, he could be suggesting that when a person begins to learn a little, and their intellectual curiosity is aroused, they become potentially dangerous, able to challenge the status quo and advance against the established order of things. It is this second potential meaning which I will consider.

Is it dangerous to learn? At the time Pope was writing many people would have argued that learning should only be for the privileged few and that a 'little learning' was dangerous in the wrong hands. In modern times however this statement would be rejected by the vast majority for several reasons. Firstly in a free and democratic country access to education is viewed as a basic human right, to learn and gain knowledge is essential to human flourishing and well-being, it would be argued that a 'little learning' is a bad thing and instead we should strive for a 'lot of learning.' Secondly in our world today there are far fewer topics of investigation and discussion which are considered 'dangerous,' we openly challenge religious, political and moral thought and we are able to do this because so many of us have received an education. Thirdly, if there is such a thing as objective truth and facts to be discovered then there is no danger from acquiring this knowledge, and acting upon it, even if that knowledge might be difficult for others to accept.

But there are still some who would agree that 'a little learning is a dangerous thing.' Particularly if we take Pope's statement more literally and suggest he is simply talking about not knowing a lot but acting as if we did. A person who has read an article on heart surgery, for example, and then carries out a triple bypass would be a considerable danger. Equally there are those who would argue that allowing the majority of people to learn and develop is a potentially dangerous thing to do. One example of this would be a population under an oppressive political regime who begin to learn a little about democracy and freedom, such learning would be considered dangerous if it meant the potential overthrow of the regime.

Acquiring knowledge through learning cannot be said to be a dangerous thing in itself it is rather how we act upon that learning which determines the danger. I might learn how to make a bomb but if I don't use that knowledge to build one and explode it in the vicinity of others then there is no danger. Likewise I might learn about revolution but if I don't go on to overthrow the government as a result then my learning is in itself not a threat. Throughout history it has been the perception of how an idea can affect those who learn it which has determined its danger. The Church suppressing theories of evolution or political parties suppressing alternative political ideas. Learning in itself can never be claimed to be a danger, but the effects of what is learned can be the most dangerous things imaginable.

It is ridiculous to treat the living body as a mechanism.

What does the above statement imply? Give examples that illustrate why it might sometimes be sensible to treat the body as a mechanisms and others that illustrate the opposite. How might you resolve this apparent contradiction?

Viewing the body as a mechanism is one way of describing how it works. The different parts fit together in an ordered manner and thus ordered they allow for a myriad of actions to take place. Each piece is essential to the whole, and if one part breaks the others suffer. The analogy to man-made mechanical devices is clear and should not be limited to human beings. For example, those who first began the study of aviation examined the make-up of birds in order to base their mechanical designs upon their anatomy – with some eventual success.

If we view the human body as a mechanism it becomes easier to understand how it functions as a whole. Take the example of running. In order to run my legs need to move in a particular way, the different muscles must interact and movement must occur. There is little difference, theoretically speaking, to the movement of an engine. In both cases a certain set of connections must exist and interact in order to produce a result: movement. Equally on the operating table the surgeon must know how the surgery upon one part of the body will affect another part. The body is a mechanism and through it different parts interact, this is particularly noticeable when a person is in pain, if the surgeon cuts into one part it will affect other parts too with visible results. In both cases treating the body as a mechanism is beneficial to understanding how and why it works.

But should the body always be treated in this way? Is it ridiculous to treat the living body as a mechanism? To argue that the body is simply a machine which reacts to different input and stimuli negates any sense of objective value, morality, aesthetic appreciation and so on. If my body is simply a machine into which different inputs are given then what more is there to life than simple mechanism? If a particular part of me can be stimulated to produce a sense of pleasure or pain then the human person is reduced only to a robot with all the ethical implications this entails. Likewise to say that the body is a mechanism, albeit a complex one, suggests a 'one size fits all approach' to many areas of medicine and research. If all bodies run along exactly the same lines, as do steam trains, then every medical problem would have the same specific solution. This is clearly not the case, we are not machines, we are individuals.

There are both benefits and disadvantages to viewing the living body as a mechanism but the contradictions between them can be resolved by taking neither to an extreme. Living bodies tend to behave in a similar way, and thus like a machine we can predict how they will react, and repair them if necessary. But unlike machines living bodies grow and develop, they interact with the world around them and when input occurs each behaves differently. Treating the body as a mechanism can have advantages in the fields of medicine but we must be wary of viewing a living body as identical to its neighbour. Unlike a machine we are the same, but different, and thus each must be treated in its own unique way using the idea of mechanism as a basic blueprint upon which to build.

Our belief in any particular natural law cannot have a safer basis than our unsuccessful critical attempts to refute it.

What do you understand by the statement above? Can you suggest examples where scientific experiment might not proceed by attempting to refute a hypothesis? To what extent do you think the statement accurately reflects the nature of scientific method?

By this statement Karl Popper suggests that when a particular natural law is examined and scrutinised, using critical methods and a degree of scepticism, and found to be correct, then we can be confident in its truth. Take the example of Isaac Newton and gravity. By considering why it is that we do not float around, but instead remain attached to the floor, the force of gravity was posited. Since every time an object is dropped it falls to the floor, rather than floating away, we can be certain that a force, known as gravity, causes this to happen. In this case a critical attempt to refute the natural law can be carried out, but in every case of attempting to refute it the law that objects thrown into the air fall to the ground will be observed.

Such an approach to scientific method is useful in demonstrating the certainty of pre-existing ideas but it is less useful in developing new scientific hypotheses. I may theorise about a particular scientific idea but if I don't have a reasonable idea as to what the result may be then constantly attempting to demonstrate it would seem futile. Only after considerable investigation and observation can a law be formulated, it is at this point that Popper's statement becomes relevant.

Such an approach can be useful in areas of science which can be said to follow certain laws, physics for example, but less so in areas such as biology. Whilst the force of gravity will always behave in the same manner here on earth, a particular species of plant or animal may not do so. A flower, for example, which has always been observed to have red flowers may suddenly develop orange flowers instead, its 'natural law' violated due to other conditions not yet catalogued. If this was the case then a new set of observations would need to be undertaken rather than the refutation of the hypothesis that all flowers of this species are red.

Equally difficulties can arise when the nature of the experiment is such that it may often produce volatile results. Take the example of chemistry. Whilst an objective natural law may exist which says that when mixing three particular chemicals together a particular reaction is observed; the quantities and ratios may be such that even the most experienced chemist only achieves the result in 10% of the experiments carried out. Whilst the theory may suggest the natural law, the initial observation may leave it open to question, the hypothesis less than demonstrable.

The scientific method is always based firstly upon observation, it is from observation that rules can be derived. If an apple falls from a tree one hundred times and hits the floor then I can reasonably suggest a natural law which claims that when an apple falls from the tree it hits the floor. But without the initial observation, and the potential errors in that observation such a law cannot be initially formulated, in science, particularly outside of physical science, exceptions to the rule can always be found as new observations are made. Whilst Popper's statement can be a useful method for proving certain scientific hypotheses as unarguably true its application to initial scientific investigation is limited, particularly in the less predictable scientific disciplines.